HSING-I KUNG-FU
VOLUME II: COMBAT
by Tim Tackett

Editor: Gregory Lee
Graphic Design: Karen Massad

Production Art: Mary Schepis

© 1983 Ohara Publications, Incorporated
All rights reserved
Printed in United States of America
Library of Congress Catalog Card No.: 75-24802
ISBN: 0-89750-084-9

Second Printing 1983

OHARA  PUBLICATIONS, INCORPORATED
BURBANK, CALIFORNIA

Dedication

To my wife, Gerry

Acknowledgements

I would like to thank Bob Chapman, John Manzano, Mark Buster and Tim Tackett, Jr., for posing for the illustrations in this book, and Linda Tackett for typing the manuscript.

About the Author

From 1962 to 1965, Tim Tackett studied Chinese boxing in Taiwan with both the mainland Chinese and native Taiwanese boxing associations. He was the first non-Chinese student to receive an instructor's certificate from the former and now holds a fifth degree black belt from the latter. While in Taiwan, Tackett studied Hsing-i kung fu, Chin Na (a Chinese art similar to aikido), Tai Chi, and both Northern and Southern Shaolin boxing. In addition, he has studied both karate and judo.

Currently, Tackett is president of the American branch of the Kuo Shu Association and is a senior jeet kune do student of Danny Inosanto in Torrance, California, and a graduate of the Filipino Kali Academy. Until this time, he has restricted his formal teaching to small, non-profit martial arts classes in Upland and Redlands, California, and occasional seminars around the country.

Tackett is married and is the father of two children. He earned a Master of Fine Arts degree in drama from the University of California where he graduated a member of *Phi Beta Kappa*. He is now an English and drama teacher at Montclair High School in Montclair, California.

This book represents the second and more advanced part of Tackett's tribute to his earliest teachers, completing his series on Hsing-i kung fu.

Introduction

This volume is a companion to my first book on the art of Hsing-i. Then, as now, it is important for the reader to remember that the study of any form of Chinese boxing is a lengthy, physically-demanding process that requires many hours of dedicated practice and concentration. If the reader has thoroughly studied and feels confident with the blocks, strikes and footwork outlined in Hsing-i Volume I, then a careful study of the advanced exercises in this book should prove helpful and enlightening.

While Volume I introduced the basic movements of Hsing-i, this volume stresses combat. Remember that these situations are just some of the infinite combinations of attack and counterattack. Preparing for 26 ways of attack is useless if your opponent knows 27. Mastering the arts of self-defense means being receptive to all the energies thrown at you and redirecting them in harmless ways.

Also included in this volume is an entire Hsing-i form, Wu Hsing, plus special breathing and tension exercises for strengthening the mind and the body. All the techniques for practice in this book can be enhanced by working with a partner.

An Explanation of Hsing-I

Hsing-i is one of the soft styles of kuo shu. Kuo shu or wu shu are the official names for Chinese boxing in both Taiwan and mainland China. Gung-fu or kung-fu is the name for Chinese boxing used in Hong Kong and means "skilled man." Kuo shu means "national sport." Whether you call Chinese boxing kung fu, ch'uan fa (fist art), or kuo shu is not important, as they are all names for the same thing.

Kuo shu has traditionally been divided into two branches, the soft and the hard styles. The hard style is called Shaolin in honor of the temple that nurtured many famous boxers. The soft styles of kuo shu are Tai Chi, Pa-kua and Hsing-i. The hard style is usually thought to rely on muscle power and meeting force with force, while the soft styles rely on the inner force, chi, and using softness to overcome strength. While this is partially true, it is not that simple. Shaolin has literally thousands of different styles and many of them are based on the use of internal power and using the opponent's own strength to defeat him.

The soft styles really differ from Shaolin in that each is based on a particular element of Chinese philosophy. Tai Chi is based on Yin and Yang. Pa-kua is based on the eight diagrams of the I Ching. Hsing-i is based on five elements of ancient Chinese philosophy. These are metal, wood, water, fire and earth. Since this book is meant to be a practical manual rather than a philosophical treatise, the five-element aspect of Hsing-i will be left out.

The true history of Hsing-i is lost in the mists of time. Both of my Hsing-i teachers claim that it was invented by Yueh Fei, a famous general of the Sung dynasty (1127-1229). It is said that Yueh Fei was a famous lance fighter and based his boxing style on the use of the lance. But all of this may be just legend.

Like many Chinese terms, Hsing-i is a difficult phrase to translate. I have heard it translated both as "form-will" or "imaginary intellectual." However it is translated, it implies that mind and body are one. You strike with your mind as well as your hand, and all parts of your body act together. When you strike with your hand you are also striking with the power of your trunk and your legs. All move as a unit.

I learned Hsing-i from two different teachers, Chen Mei Shou and Yuan Tao. As a young man, Chen learned Hsing-i in both Taiwan and in Fukien province on the mainland. Yuan Tao, a former guerrilla general, learned his Hsing-i from the famous Wu Yun-t'ing on the mainland of China.

One of the most noticeable aspects of this book is the number of variations that the original, formal stances assume. Chen is probably the greatest influence here, with his unorthodox approach to Hsing-i and his practical outlook on what a stance should be. From the basic, formal positions, he encouraged whatever modifications that assisted the hand movements and added speed and power to their delivery. Such modifications included transferring the weight to the lead foot to assist the forward motion on a strike, angling the body for better power and accuracy and pivoting one or both feet to "launch" the hands. My training under Danny Inosanto further convinced me that these modifications were both valid and even necessary in practical applications, and so they will be included throughout the book.

—Tim Tackett
Redlands, California
1982

Contents

Stretching

Stretching is as important in Hsing-i as in any other martial art. The tendons, so important in the conceptual approach to Hsing-i, need to be flexed daily to their maximum, allowing your body the fullest range of motion during practice.

Be sure to perform each stretch fully and to hold them for at least 30 seconds each, repeating the sequence of stretches twice to make sure you are as limber as possible. In a matter of weeks, the increased extension will become apparent to you, especially when applied in the tension exercises and heavy arm training which follow in Chapter Two.

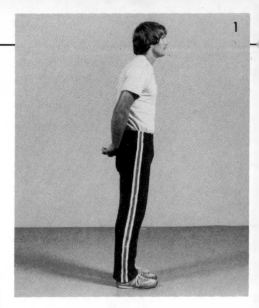

STANDING STRETCH

(1&2) From an erect position, bend forward at the waist while simultaneously extending your arms behind your back and up in a slow arc. Your head approaches your knees as your arms and hands reach higher until you can go no further. Move into this stretch slowly and hold it for 30 seconds or more. Breathe evenly. Now bring your arms down (3) in a slow arc and grasp behind your ankles, gently tugging your torso forward as far as possible. Hold.

SITTING DOUBLE LEG STRETCH

From a sitting position, legs extended, grasp your ankles and reach as far as you can, pulling your head and torso slowly forward until you can touch your knees. Hold.

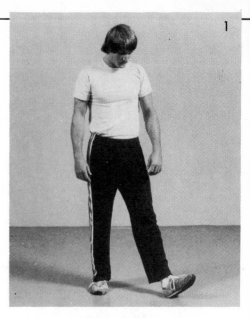

STANDING SINGLE
LEG STRETCH

(1) From a standing position place your left foot forward about one foot, heel resting lightly on the ground and toes pointed up. Reach down (2) by grasping your ankle with both hands and pulling your head gently to your left knee. Repeat this stretch (3&4) with the right leg and hold.

ROLLBACK STRETCH

(1) From a sitting position, knees bent, roll backward and raise your feet over your head until your toes touch (2) the ground in back of you. Keep your hands firmly on your knees and begin to push up on them to fully extend your legs in a stretch. Breath evenly and hold this for 30 seconds. Return to the starting position slowly and repeat.

LEG SPLITS

(1) Spread your feet as wide apart as possible, and press straight down on your thighs with your hands. (2) Now sink down into a complete split on the floor and reach out toward your left ankle,

pulling your head to your left knee. Move slowly to your right (3&4), pulling your head to the ground between your legs and gradually reaching your right ankle and knee. Repeat and hold.

Chi Training

Chi is a form of energy that all living creatures possess. To use chi in combat, however, you must nurture it and know how to control it. Nurturing the chi with Hsing-i training will make your arms feel heavy and allow you to block attacks with a relaxed motion. After Hsing-i heavy arm training, your strength is seated in your tendons rather than your muscles and your blocks and strikes will be much stronger than they would be with normal muscular strength.

There is a point in your training, which differs with every individual, when your arms will start to feel very weak. This feeling will last anywhere from two weeks to one month. Then your arms will start to feel very heavy and the power of your blocks and strikes will be much stronger than if you tried to use just your muscles.

To develop the Hsing-i chi you must follow all the instructions given and do the proper number of repetitions every day for at least two years.

While two of the breathing exercises are from the tai chi shaolin school, they were used by one of my teachers to help build chi.

FLAT WALK
BREATHING EXERCISE

(1) Stand with your heels together, your feet at 45-degree angles and your knees slightly bent. Arrange your hands in a short flat walk position, raising your left hand so that the first knuckle of your index finger is even with your nose, and lowering your right hand so that it touches your abdomen. Your index fingers should be pointing at the ceiling and your remaining fingers turned upward as much as possible. From the starting position, breathe in slowly and evenly through your nose by expanding your lower stomach. Do not move your chest. While inhaling, focus your eyes on your index finger and concentrate on a point about one-and-a-half inches below your navel. Exhale through your nose while imagining that your breath is moving up your body, through your left arm and out your palm. Lead your breath with your mind and try to relax as much as possible. Repeat the sequence a second time. On your third inhalation (2&3) turn your palms outward with the fingers of your right hand pointing downward and your thumbs separated from your fingers in a grasping attitude. As you inhale, tense your arms slightly and push them slowly away from the front of your body until they are even with your sides. Bring your hands to your waist (4) closing them into fists with your palms down, just as you complete one full inhalation. Your elbows should be pressed inward at this point, stretching your pectoral muscles. Then execute a right uppercut (5&6) with the palms of both fists turned up, your right fist extended and your left fist pressed firmly against the side of your right arm, just below the bicep. You should ex-

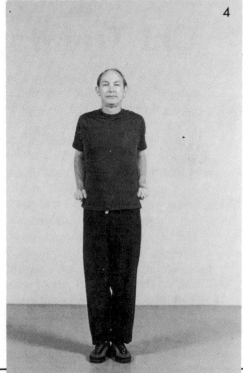

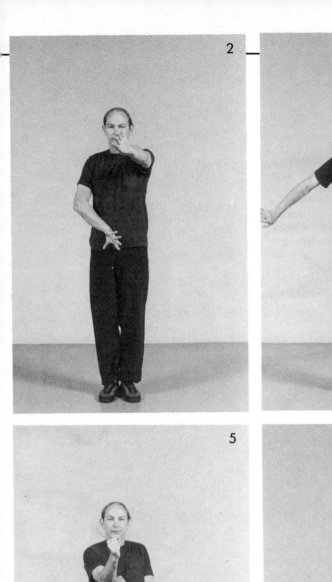

Continued on next page

hale half of your air through your nose as you punch and try to lead your fist with your mind. While still holding your breath (7) open both fists. Very slowly, with as little tension as possible, circle your left hand down (8-11), back and up over your head. Do not move your right arm. While exhaling the rest of your breath (12&13) drop both hands slowly to the starting position.

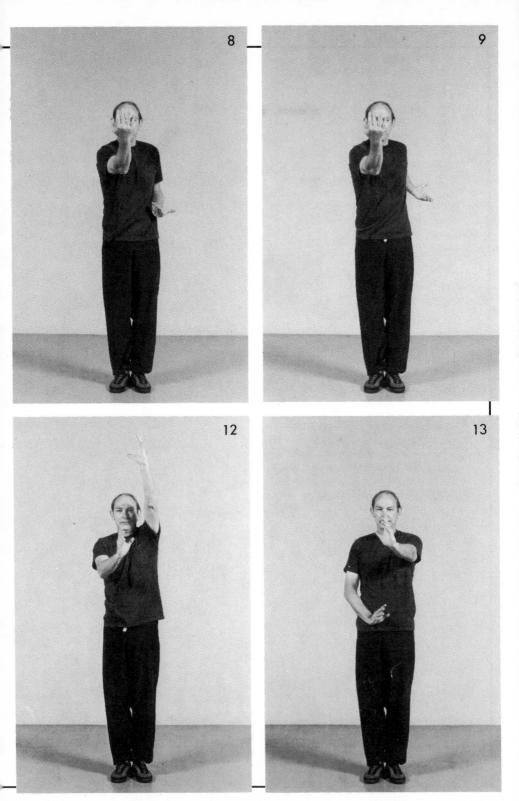

TENSION EXERCISE #1

Assume a horse stance (1) and hold your fists tensely in front of you at shoulder level with your palms facing each other about six inches apart. Inhale and exhale slowly through your nose by expanding and contracting your lower stomach. Then (2&3) inhale quickly as you drop your fists to your hips. Open your hands (4) into willow leaf palms and draw them up along your sides to your chest. Strike forward (5&6) with the fingertips of both hands while exploding your breath out through your nose. While

Continued on next page

inhaling slowly (7-11) tense your entire body and further tense your arms by bending your palms toward you, turning your fingers downward and slowly circling them to the outside and on around until they point upward, with your palms facing forward. Finally (12&13) clench your hands into fists and bring them to their original position while completely exhaling through your nose, at the same time tightening the muscles throughout your body.

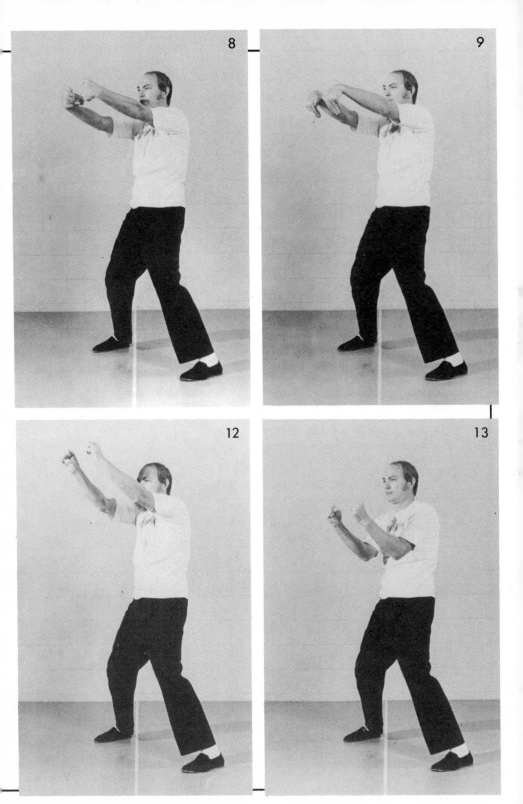

TENSION EXERCISE #2

Assume a horse stance (1) and hold your hands in front of you at shoulder level with the heels of your hands about six inches apart and with your palms and fingers angled outward at 45 degrees. Spread your fingers to add stress to the muscles in your wrists. Breathe in slowly through your nose by expanding your lower stomach. Then (2) inhale quickly as you lower your hands to the front of your thighs with your palms facing downward. Draw your hands upward (3) along your body until your palms are facing your chest and your elbows are raised to shoulder level. Next (4) strike forward with the fingertips of both hands while exploding your breath out through your nose. Finally (5&6) return your hands to their original position while tensing all the muscles in your body.

HEAVY ARM TRAINING

Stand in a horse stance (1) with a bean bag or a stack of magazines on a table in front of you. Open your right hand (2&3) and circle it back and above your head. While keeping your arm relaxed and slightly bent (4&5) slap the palm of your hand down heavily while dropping your body weight slightly upon contact to add power. Lift your hand (6) off the striking pad and across your body. Then raise your hand up (7-9) in a circular backhand motion and drop it, striking with the back of your hand. Repeat your first motion (10-13) striking with

Continued on next page

the blade of your hand. Finally (14-22) repeat the entire exercise with your left hand. This exercise will provide your hands with the toughening resistance and strength they need to become more powerful with Hsing-i techniques. The process is continual and requires stamina. This one exercise will gradually give you a feeling of control and power in your hands.

Arm Boxing

Arm boxing is not only used to harden the arms, but in its succeeding stages it can be used as a long-term training method to cultivate heavy arm tendon strength. This chapter contains a three-year training program.

Beginning with the first stage, perform these exercises every other day for six months. Hit softly at first and build up to full power in one or two months. Three hits on one arm is a complete set. Try to do at least ten sets for each arm when you first begin training.

When you get so that you are doing the exercises at full power, arm box until your arms become numb, then do five more sets on each arm.

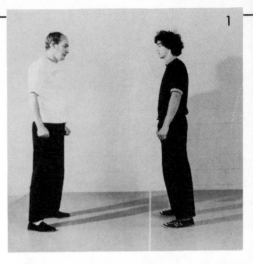

FIRST STAGE, FIRST SEQUENCE

Stand facing your partner (1) about four feet away with your fists clenched and your arm muscles tensed. One person should step forward (2-4) with his right foot as the other steps back with his left, and then both should swing their right arms out and down with knuckles turned inward so that their arms hit together on the muscle just below the elbow. Your arms should hit and stick without bouncing off each other. Then (5) separate and drop your arms straight down. Arc your right arms up (6&7) and across your bodies, leading with your knuckles and bringing your forearms together above your heads so that you are striking on the same part of both arms. Finally (8-10) swing your arms down and across your bodies, leading with your knuckles so that you accomplish a second low strike and complete the sequence.

38

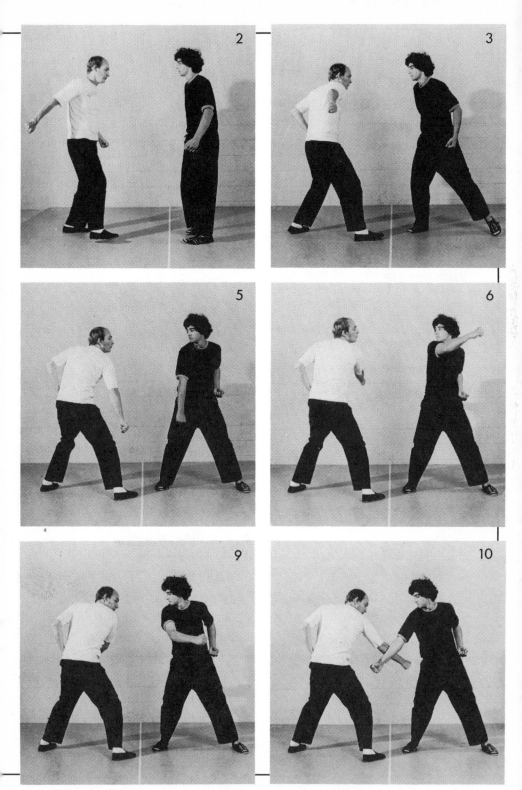

FIRST STAGE, SECOND SEQUENCE

The second sequence begins (1) at the end of the first sequence. Both partners should (2) swing their left arms back as one person steps forward with his left foot and the other steps back with his right. Then both should swing their left arms around and down with knuckles turned inward so that the arms hit (3&4) together on the muscular part of the forearm just below the elbow. The same strike is then repeated (5-7) in an upward position and then again (8-10) in a downward position.

SECOND STAGE

The first and second sequences of the second stage are identical to those in the first stage, except that one man will keep his hand open and his arm relaxed for ten sets. He will then tighten his arm and clench his fist while his partner performs ten sets openhanded.

Second stage arm boxing should begin after six months of training in the first stage and should continue every other day for six months.

An important point to remember while doing the openhanded half of second stage arm boxing is to keep your arm relaxed and imagine that it is very heavy. By doing this your arm will hit harder and last longer than the person using muscular strength.

SECOND STAGE, FIRST SEQUENCE

Stand facing your partner (1) about four feet apart with your fists clenched and your arm muscles tensed. One person (2) steps forward with his right foot while the other (3) steps back with his left. Both men swing their right arms forward and meet (4) in a lowered arm position at the muscle just below the elbow. Then (5&6) from an upper arm position both men (7) swing their arms down and meet once again (8) in a lowered arm position.

SECOND STAGE, SECOND SEQUENCE

From a relaxed stance one man (1) steps forward with his left foot while the other (2) steps back with his right. Then (3) both swing their left arms forward and meet in a lowered arm position at the muscle just below the elbow. Next (4&5) they meet in an upper arm position and finally (6&7) in a lowered arm position.

THIRD STAGE

The first and second sequences of the third stage are identical to the second stage, except that you will notice the third strike of each set is done with the inside of both men's forearms. With the third sequence included, the entire third stage should be practiced with the second stage by alternating them every day for one year.

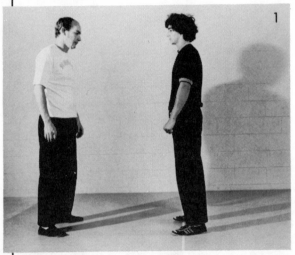

THIRD STAGE, FIRST SEQUENCE

Begin (1) in a relaxed position about four feet apart. Then (2-4) as one man steps forward with his right foot and the other

steps back with his left, both men swing their right arms forward and meet in a lowered arm position at

Continued on next page

the muscle just below the elbow. Next (5-7) they meet in an upper arm position and finally (8-10)

in a lowered arm position. Notice that the last strike is executed with both men's inner arms.

Note: The second sequence of the third stage is exactly the same as the first sequence, except that it is executed with the left arm.

THIRD STAGE, THIRD SEQUENCE

At the end of the second sequence when both men have their left foot and arm forward (1) both should raise their right hand to ear level with palms facing outward. The man who ended the second sequence with a closed fist will keep his fist closed and the other's will remain open. As one man steps back with his left foot and the other steps forward with his

right (2&3) their right arms should remain bent and they should swing them around at shoulder level so that they strike each other on the inside of the forearm just below the elbow. Finally (4-6) as one man steps back with his right foot and the other steps forward with his left, both men should swing their left arms back and around at shoulder level, hitting the same way.

FOURTH STAGE

During your third year of heavy arm training, continue alternating the second and third stages and add daily practice in the fourth stage.

The two sequences of the fourth stage are identical to those in the first stage, except that the striking points are the backs of the wrists. Your arms should remain relaxed and your hand should snap back upon contact, locking with your partner's wrist.

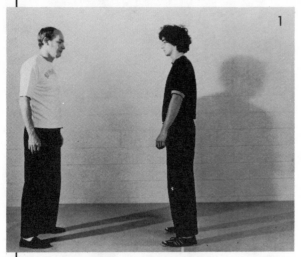

FOURTH STAGE, FIRST SEQUENCE

Begin (1) in a relaxed position about four feet apart from each other. Then (2-4) as one man steps forward

with his right foot and the other steps back with his left, both men swing their arms forward to a lowered

Continued on next page

arm position, striking each other on the back of the wrist. Next (5-7) they move to an upper arm

position and finally (8-10) back to a lowered arm position.

Note: The second sequence is identical to the first, except that it is executed with the left arm.

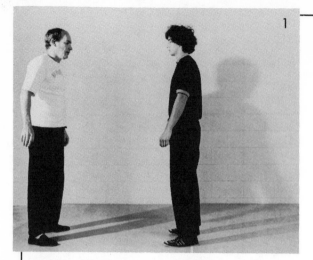

FIFTH STAGE

Fifth stage arm box-
ing should begin after
two-and-a-half years of
heavy arm training and
it should be alternated
with the second and
third stages, replacing
the fourth stage every
other day.

FIFTH STAGE,
FIRST SEQUENCE

Begin (1) in a relaxed position about four feet apart
from each other. Then (2-3)
as one man steps forward
with his right foot and the
other steps back with his
left, they strike each other
with the back of their right

At the end of three years your arms should feel heavy and you should be able to block and hit with great power while you are relaxed. Continue the heavy arm boxing every other day.

wrists in a lowered arm position then in a (4&5) raised arm position and finally in a (6) lowered arm position once again, striking on the inner portion of their wrists.

FIFTH STAGE, SECOND SEQUENCE

Both men (1) have struck each other on the back of the wrist in the lowered arm position. Then (2&3) they swing their arms up to strike each other in the

upper arm position and finally (4&5) back to the lowered arm position where they strike each other on the inner portion of their wrists.

FIFTH STAGE, THIRD SEQUENCE

Both men (1) have struck each other on the inside of their left wrists in the lowered arm position with their right arms raised to head level. Next (2&3) one man steps forward with his right foot while the other steps back with his left while they swing their right arms forward to

3

strike each other on the inside of the wrist in an upper arm position at head level. Finally (4) one man advances again while the other retreats and they swing their left arms forward to strike each other on the inside of the wrist in an upper arm position at head level.

4

Wu Hsing Form One

Although there are many forms of Hsing-i, the first is the most important because it builds both chi and strong legs. The form is comprised of the five basic hands of Hsing-i. All the footwork and hand strikes have been explained in Volume I. This form is similar to the first form taught to me by Yuan Tao, but I have selected Chen Mei Shou's form over the other because it is easier to follow in still photographs.

Follow the breathing directions closely wherever they become specific. Otherwise, breathe slowly when flowing from one move to the next and explode your breath out when striking.

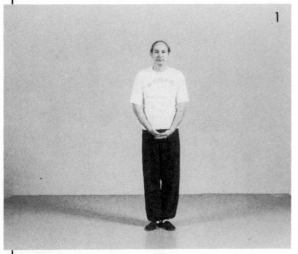

WU HSING
BREATHING SALUTE

Stand with your heels together (1), your feet at a 45-degree angle. Your arms hang naturally with your open hands cupped, palms up, in front of you with your right hand on top of your left. Inhale and exhale twice in this position (2) as you did in the breathing exercise earlier. As you inhale the third

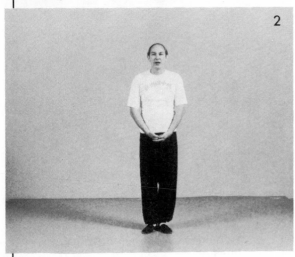

time, raise your arms (3) away from your side, cupping them over your head (4), left hand over your right and palms down, just as you reach full inhalation. Hold this position for two seconds. Then, keeping your hands together, slowly lower them in front of you (5) and bend your

Continued on next page

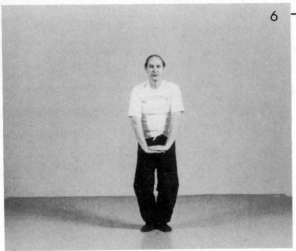

knees slightly (6) as you exhale. Your arms should reach full lower extension as you complete your exhalation. Inhale quickly (7) and explode your breath out through your nose as you execute a right uppercut with the palms of both fists turned upward, your right fist extended and your left fist pressed firm-

ly against the side of your right forearm, just above the elbow. Next (8) open your hands. Slowly and gently, inhale (9) as you raise your left leg and arm. Slowly exhale (10&11) as you lower your hands into a left flat walk smash and your left leg into a left short flat walk stance.

FIRST SEQUENCE

(1) From the last position of the breathing salute, perform the first two breaths of the flat walk breathing exercise explained earlier in Chapter Two. (2-4) Perform the third breath of the flat walk breathing exercise while stepping forward with your left foot into a long flat walk stance and simultaneously executing a left uppercut with your hands in a flat walk position. With the punch, exhale only one-half of your breath. (5) Raise your right hand back and above your head as you step forward (6) into a right short flat walk stance, hands open.

Continued on next page

(7) Exhale completely as you smash down as hard and as fast as possible to the opposite of position #1 with your right hand on top. (8-13) *Repeat* the sequence on the opposite side. Now *repeat* the entire sequence on your left and right sides a second time (not shown). Step back six to ten

Continued on next page

inches with your right foot and pivot 90 degrees clockwise (14&15) on the balls of your feet until you are in a horse stance, while placing your fists, palms down, against your hips. Slide the right foot back (16) toward your left foot and step directly to your right (17) into a right long flat walk stance and execute a right uppercut with your hands in a flat walk position, while exhaling one-half of your breath. (18-20) Step forward with a left short flat walk stance and slide your right foot to your left while opening your hands and raising your left hand back and above your head. Exhale completely as you execute another flat walk smash as hard and as fast as possible with your left hand on top. Inhale and exhale twice in this last position.

Continued on next page

SECOND SEQUENCE

The third time you inhale, execute a slow, tense elbow block (21&22), palm up, on your left side while sliding your left foot back until your heel touches your right foot. While expelling one-half of your breath, take a quick step with your left foot (23) into a long flat walk stance and execute a left upward finger strike. Step forward with your right foot (24) while executing a downward palm block with your left hand and position your right fist in front of your chest, palm up, with your forearm at a 45-degree angle rising away from you. (25) Slide your left foot slowly behind your right into a right short flat walk stance, close your left hand into a fist, palm down at your belt, and deliver a quick right uppercut while expelling the rest of your breath. (Take three breaths while in this last position.) (26-30) Repeat steps 21-25 (this first part of the second sequence) on the opposite side, keeping the palm closed, then a sec-

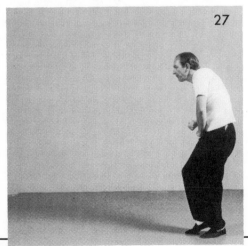

Continued on next page

ond time on the left side. Now (31) step back six to ten inches with your right foot and pivot 90 degrees clockwise on the balls of your feet until you are in a horse stance, while placing your fists palms down against your hips. Inhale as you enter the horse stance. Hit to the right with a reverse small tiger's mouth (32) while expelling one-third of your breath. Circle your right arm (33) over and around your head in a clockwise motion, bringing your right hand to your right shoulder palm forward, and make a 90-degree turn to your right, sliding your right foot back (34) into a right cat stance. Step forward (35) into a right long flat walk stance and execute a right upward finger strike while expelling one-third of your breath. Step forward into a left short flat walk stance, drop your right hand in a fist palm down in front of you, and execute a left uppercut (36&37) while expelling the rest of your breath. (Inhale and exhale twice while in this final position.)

Continued on next page

THIRD SEQUENCE

As you inhale a third time, straighten your left arm into a vertical punch position (38) and draw your right fist, palm in, to your hip. (39-41) Step forward with your left foot and slide your right foot forward into another left short flat walk stance as you expel your breath and simultaneously execute a right vertical punch over your left hand while drawing your left hand back to your hip. (42-44) Step and slide to a third left short flat walk stance while executing a left vertical punch. (45&46) Repeat your step and execute another right vertical punch.

Continued on next page

(47) Jerk your right fist back to your hip executing an elbow strike to the rear. The heels of both fists should be touching your hips. (48-51) Pivot 180 degrees clockwise on your heels and execute simultaneously a right Hsing-i kick and a right uppercut, your left fist pressed against your right arm just above the elbow. Open your hands, draw your right elbow to your side and raise your left hand above your head. Stomp your right foot down while executing a downward flat walk smash with your left hand. (52-53) Raise your right foot again and stomp down six inches forward. Step forward into a right long flat walk stance. (54-55) Slide your left foot into an entering tiger stance and execute a right vertical punch, drawing your left fist back to your hip, palm in.

Continued on next page

FOURTH SEQUENCE

(56-58) While pulling your right fist back to your hip, palm in, sidestep 45 degrees to your left and draw into a right cat stance, facing 45 degrees to your right. As you sidestep, inhale. While in the cat stance, exhale slowly and pause for two seconds, then inhale slowly and pause for two seconds. (59&60) Step 45 degrees to your right and quickly draw your left foot up into an entering tiger stance. At the same time, block overhead with your right arm and execute a left vertical punch while forcefully expelling your breath. (61-66) Repeat the movements on the opposite side so that you finish in an entering tiger stance with a left overhead block and a right

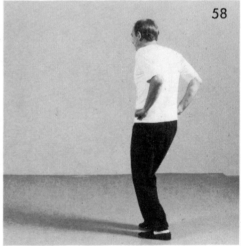

Continued on next page

vertical punch. Repeat a second time on both sides, alternately (not shown). (67-70) With your left foot, step across and in front of your right foot, a shoulder's width to your right, while pivoting 180 degrees clockwise on your right foot. At the same time, lift your right fist away from your side to shoulder height while drawing your left fist to your hip. Pivot 45 degrees to your right on your left foot while drawing your right foot back into a cat stance. At the same time, inhale as you circle your arm clockwise in front of you to block at face level with your forearm. Keep your fist clenched with your palm toward you.

FIFTH SEQUENCE

(71-73) Step forward with your right foot while executing a left circular block, drawing your right fist, palm in, to your hip. Quickly draw your left foot up into an entering tiger stance and execute a left back knuckle (74) while forcefully expelling your breath. Repeat the footwork for steps 58-62, but on the opposite side (not shown), facing the opposite direction. Repeat steps 71-74 again, alternating left and right at 45-degree angles once more until you are in the same position as 74. (75) Sidestep with your right foot and pivot (76) on your left foot 180 degrees clockwise into a left cat stance and draw your left fist (77) to your hip, palm up. (78-81) Step forward with your left foot into a long flat walk stance and execute a left uppercut with your hands in the flat

Continued on next page

walk position. Circle your right hand down, back and above your head as you step forward with your right foot. Slide your left foot to your right into a right short flat walk stance and execute (82) a downward flat walk smash with your right hand. (83-89) Step forward with your right foot and repeat the movements on the opposite side. Then (90-96) repeat again

Continued on next page

steps 78-82. (97&98) Step forward with your right foot and pivot 90 degrees counterclockwise into a horse stance while drawing both fists to your hips, palms down. (99) Turn 90 degrees counterclockwise and draw your left foot back into a cat stance. (100) Step forward with your left foot into a long flat walk stance and execute a left uppercut with your hands while forcefully expelling your

Continued on next page

breath. (101) As you begin to step forward with your right foot, open your hands. (102) Inhale as you raise your right leg and circle your right hand down, back and over your head. (103) Exhale as you slowly execute a right downward flat walk smash and lower your leg into a right short flat walk stance. (104&105) Step back with your right foot and draw your left foot to your right, place your heels together with your feet pointing 45 degrees outward. (106-110) Repeat steps 1-5 of the breathing salute. (111) Finish.

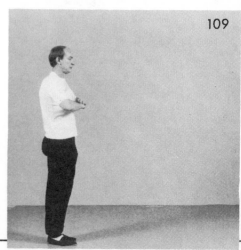

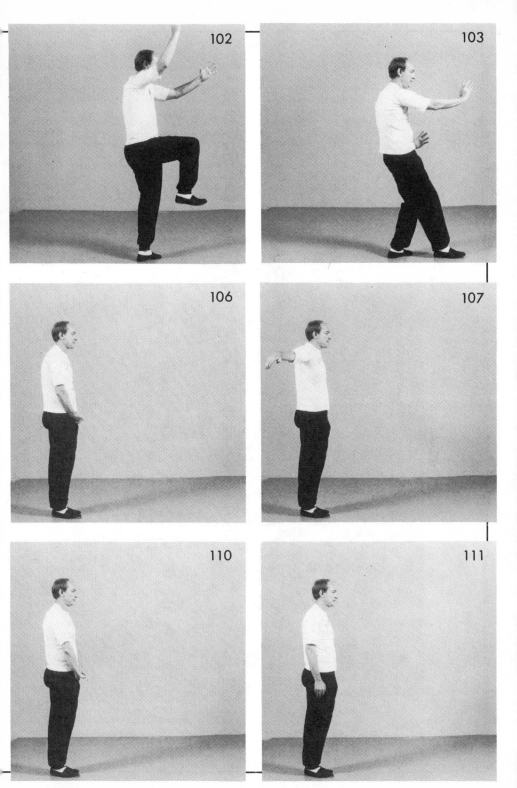

Self-Defense Awareness

Probably one of the most important aspects of self-defense in Hsing-i is proper distance. Whenever possible, you should stand just out of reach of your opponent's kicks and punches so he will have to step forward before he is close enough to deliver a strike. By keeping this distance, my teachers felt that a man who attacks would be opening himself up to a counterattack. Both advised me that if I were ever threatened, I should relax and let my opponent make the first move. Chen Mei Shou's students took this advice so literally that sparring matches were very boring to watch. I have seen two students stand and face each other for as long as ten minutes without moving, until one couldn't stand it any longer and would attack. The great majority of the time, the first person to move would lose.

Proper eye contact is also important. Many karate and kung fu teachers believe you should watch your opponent's eyes when you are in a combat situation. My teachers felt that this had two disadvantages. The first problem is the tendency to lose sight of your opponent's feet. Then, too, a clever boxer or streetfighter can fake with his eyes by looking one way and hitting another. If you focus on your opponent's solar plexus, you can see both his arms and legs with your peripheral vision, and it is harder for him to fake you.

It should be mentioned here that kicking is also an important part of Hsing-i self-defense, often neglected because of its simplicity. Though all Hsing-i kicks are kept relatively low, they are excellent tools, especially for defense. Because the leg is longer than the arm, a kick can stop almost any hand attack when properly timed. Your legs can also be used to jam your opponent's kick when he attacks or to block your lower areas when you are attacking.

And finally, if you should ever encounter a combat situation, don't try to anticipate your opponent's moves. Let your mind float freely, relax and let your body react. Before your body can react properly, however, it must be trained. Knowing how to block and punch will not make you block and punch as a reaction. The following section will provide the practice necessary to develop the automatic movements you need in self-defense. Once you have learned them, continue to practice them to keep your reflexes sharp.

SLIPPING INSIDE

Face your partner (1) and assume a natural stance to his horse stance. As he executes a right face level punch (2) pivot 90 degrees counterclockwise into a left extended flat walk stance while leaning back on your right leg and executing a right side palm to his face. As he executes a left face level punch (3&4) pivot 180 degrees clockwise into a

right extended flat walk stance while leaning back on your left leg and executing a left side palm to his face. Keep repeating this drill (5) as he continues to punch. Once you have become familiar with the movement, your partner should return his fist to his hip after each punch and not let you know which hand he will punch with next.

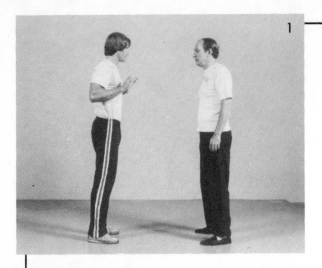

SLIPPING OUTSIDE

Face your partner (1) and assume a natural stance to his horse stance. As he executes a left face level punch (2) pivot 90 degrees counterclockwise into a left extended flat walk stance while leaning back on your right leg and executing (3) a right one knuckle punch to his ribs.

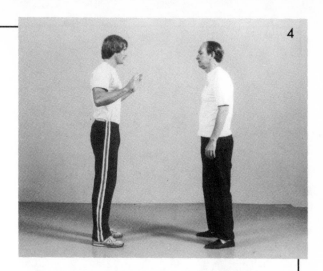

As he executes a right face level punch (4&5) pivot 180 degrees clockwise into a right extended flat walk stance while leaning back on your left leg and executing (6) a left one knuckle punch to his ribs. Keep repeating this drill.

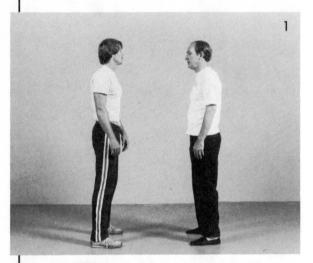

WEAVING

Face your partner (1) and assume a natural stance. As he begins a right roundhouse punch to your head (2) lean your body slightly to your right. As his punch arcs forward

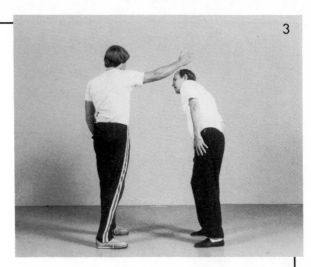

3

4

(3&4) bend at the waist and move your head beneath his punch and to your left. As you lift your head on the outside of his punch (5&6) twist your

5

Continued on next page

6

7

shoulders counterclockwise and execute a right palm smash to his groin. Then (7) look for his returning punch. As he executes a left roundhouse punch to your head (8) bend at the waist and move your head beneath

his punch and to your right. As you lift your head on the outside of his punch (9&10) twist your shoulders clockwise and execute a left palm smash to his 'groin. Keep repeating this drill.

DROPPING BACK

Assume a right stance (1) to your partner's left stance and keep your hands at your sides. As your partner steps forward (2&3) with a right face punch, rock your upper torso back and out of his

range while lifting the ball of your right foot up. Simultaneously execute an upward palm block with your right hand. (4&5) Follow up the elbow block with a kick to the armpit.

SIDESTEPPING DRILLS

In the following drill you and your partner will practice stepping outside a direct frontal attack, learning to flow in the opposite direction from the punch and repeating the drill many times without knowing which of your partner's hands is going to try and

STEPPING OUTSIDE

(1) You and your partner face each other in a natural stance, your hands by your sides and his hands near his chest, palms facing you. (2) As your partner steps forward to push you with his left hand, step to the outside of his arm with your right foot, drawing your left foot in front of your right (3) into a left extended flat walk stance and execute a double circular block. Return to the first position

punch you.

You may also practice the same drill by stepping to the inside, where your opponent still has two hands to use against you, but his groin is open to a front kick and his stance is weaker.

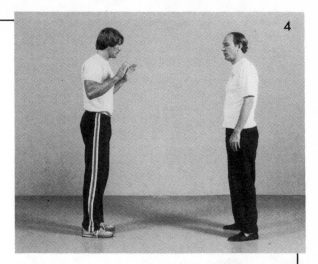

(4) and repeat the same drill, with your partner trying to push you with his right hand (5) while you step to the outside with the left foot and execute a double circular block (6). This time, you are facing him in a right extended flat walk stance. *Note:* By stepping to the outside, you have "zoned off" his opposite hand. His balance, however, is somewhat stronger than if you were inside.

ABSORPTION DRILL

Assume a right short flat walk stance (1) to your partner's left stance and keep your hands at your sides. As he steps forward (2&3) with his right foot and delivers a right punch, bend at the waist and rock back with the punch. Timing is important here. Let the punch hit you slightly as you tighten your stomach and forcefully expel your air. If you move back too soon,

the drill accomplishes nothing and in actual combat your face would receive the blow. If you move back too late, you will receive the full power of the blow. Have your partner start with light punches and then work up to full power. As a counter in a real situation, a right flat walk smash can be executed (4&5) after the initial punch.

AWARENESS DRILL

Stand naturally (1) looking straight ahead with your partner at a 45-degree angle in front of you. Then (2) allow him to step forward with a punch at any time that suits him. Block and counter (3) while keeping your eyes straight ahead. Use only your peripheral vision. As you master this, have your partner vary his attacks, using his hands or feet.

When you can block anything he throws and explode into a counterattack, have him move to your side. Eventually, he should be able to walk out of your peripheral vision and you will still be able to defend by listening for his attack or by noticing changes in the general sound of air pressure around you.

CIRCULAR BLOCK AND TRAP DRILL #1

(1) You and your partner face each other in right fighting stances. When your partner executes a high right punch (2) deflect it to the outside (3) with a right circular block, palm forward. Lower his arm to waist level (4) and grab. Execute a hand change (5-7) and deflect his arm outside to the left. As you begin to execute a high right punch (8&9) at your

Continued on next page

Continued from preceding page

partner, he will deflect it (10&11) to his outside with a right circular block, lowering your arm to waist level (12) and grabbing the wrist. Next he will execute a hand change (13&14). As he begins his high right punch again (15-18), repeat the entire sequence. Do this repeatedly and then begin the drill using the left hand to punch.

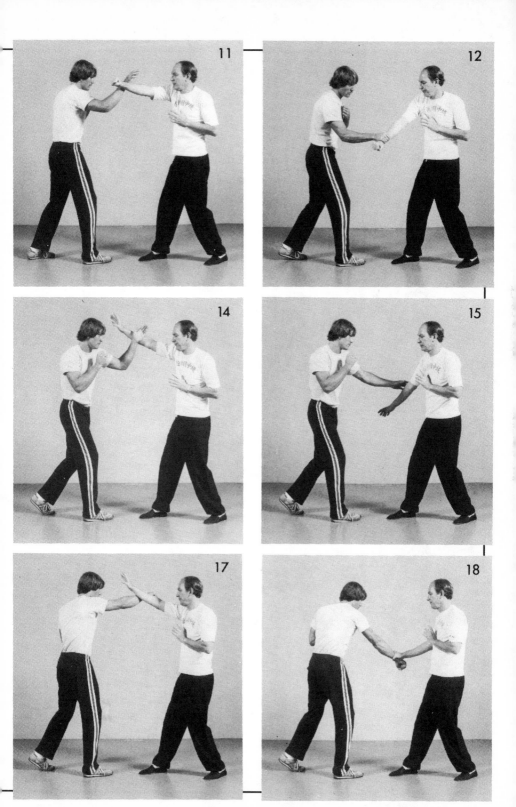

CIRCULAR BLOCK AND TRAP DRILL #2

(1) You and your partner face each other in right fighting stances. As your partner executes a high right punch (2) deflect it to the inside with a left circular block and trap, your palm pushing his elbow. Bring your right

hand underneath his right arm and your left (3) and continue to deflect his right punch across your body with back of your right arm pushing against his (4). Grab (5) his wrist with your right hand and

Continued on next page

bring your left arm under (6) and deflect his right arm back (7) to the outside. As you begin to throw a high right punch

(8), your partner will repeat the inside circular block (9-11). Do this drill alternately with left and right punches.

Advanced Self-Defense Drills

It must be remembered that self-defense is a spontaneous thing and an attack must be dealt with as it takes place rather than by trying to plan out your moves. The self-defense techniques that follow describe some common situations and effective defenses for them. They are by no means the only way to handle those particular situations. By learning them, however, you will build a base from which to launch your own investigations.

KICKING DRILL #1

(1) Begin in a right short flat walk stance and hold your hands in a modified flat walk position, with the right hand palm up and your left hand in a relaxed position near your solar plexus. Your hands should assume this position at the end of each circular block to follow. Next, execute (2&3) a right front kick. Begin a left circular block (4&5) as you step to your right and pivot 90 degrees counterclockwise to assume a left short flat walk stance (6). Now execute a left front kick (7&8). Plant

Continued on next page

your left foot (9) while pivoting 180 degrees clockwise (10), executing a right circular block and ending (11) in a right short flat walk stance. (12&13) Execute a right front kick. Step directly to your left with the right foot, execute a left circular block (14) as you pivot 180 degrees counterclockwise and assume a left short flat walk stance (15). Finally, execute a left front kick (16). Note how the kicks alternate with the left and right foot as you kick in the four directions.

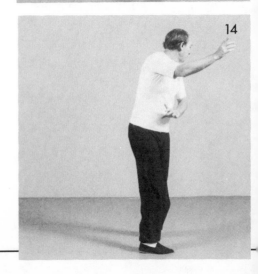

KICKING DRILL #2

(1) Assume the starting position of kicking drill #1 and execute (2&3) a right front kick. Step forward (4) with your right foot and execute a left hook kick (5&6). Set your left foot

Continued on next page

down (7) and execute a right side kick (8&9). Set the right foot down (10) into your original starting position and execute a back kick (11&12) with your left foot.

STICKY HANDS PRACTICE

These drills are designed to develop your ability to follow and make use of your opponent's energy. They are very important and must be mastered before you begin trapping hands practice. Master each drill before going on to the next and learn to flow from one drill to another.

ROLLING HANDS

Assume a right stance (1) to your partner's right stance and place your right wrist on top of his right wrist. Push forward while your partner rocks

After mastering a drill, try it with your eyes closed to develop the proper sensitivity. Treat the exercise like a game and don't worry about being hit. Strength is not important during these drills, so start slowly and gradually pick up speed.

back (2&3) with your energy, lifting the toes of his front foot and raising his arm in front of his body. He then circles your arm to his outside (4&5)

Continued on next page

and pushes your hand away. As he begins to push on top of your wrist (6), repeat the same motions, rocking back and circling his wrist (7-9) to

7

8

the outside. Continue this rolling back-and-forth motion and then repeat the drill alternately with the left hands.

9

SLAPPING SHOULDER

Assume a left stance (1) to your partner's left stance and place the back of your left wrist against the back of his left wrist. As you try to slap his left shoulder (2) he will deflect your motion to his left outside. When he tries to slap your left

4

5

shoulder (3&4) deflect his motion to your left side. Repeat. Once you have mastered the drill, try occasionally to unbalance your opponent by grabbing his wrist (5&6) as you redirect it and pull him to your rear.

6

TWO COUNT

Assume a right stance (1) to your partner's right stance and place the back of your right wrist against the back of his right wrist. Your partner (2&3) will attempt to lower your wrist and spring up for a face attack. Instead (4-6) relax and follow his upward energy while adding to it to direct his strike above your head. Don't lose contact with his wrist. At

Continued on next page

the highest point turn your palm outward and push downward (7&8) to attempt a similar face attack. He
should counter your attack the same
way you countered his, by lifting up
(9). After you have practiced two-
count attacks (10) try just dropping
your hand from the defense position
to deliver a direct chop to your partner's side. Your partner should defend
(11&12) by dropping his right elbow
while clinging to your wrist and
shooting upward for a face attack.

TWO COUNT FLOW

Assume the right fighting stance (1) with your right wrists together as in the previous two count exercise. Grab and push (2) your partner's wrist down, then shoot upward (3) for a face attack. Your partner defends by following your energy upward and deflecting the strike past his head. Before he can

counterattack, arc your hand downward for a chop to the side (4). He should follow your movement downward by dropping his elbow and then attempt a face attack. Deflect it (5) in the same manner as your partner did. Repeat for both hands, and try to maintain wrist contact.

SMALL DISENGAGEMENT DRILL

Begin (1) in the starting position of the two count drill. Then (2-4) as your partner attempts to push your hand across your body, pivot your hand down and around to the in-

3

4

side of his wrist so you are pushing his wrist in the direction of his original motion with the blade of your hand. Spring off his arm (5) and deliver a chop to his neck. His defense

5

Continued on next page

motion (6-8) would be to dissolve your chop by following and assisting your motion by clinging to your wrist and pushing it to his left side. He would then attempt a chop (9-11) and you would defend in the same

way. To return to your original position, apply your small disengagement movement in reverse, so that you pivot your wrist to the outside of your partner's wrist.

LARGE DISENGAGEMENT DRILL

Begin in the same starting position (1) as the small disengagement drill. Your partner's objective is to push your arm across your body and down (2&3) and strike with an upward palm heel. Instead, move your arm in a counterclockwise circle (4-7) and strike his temple with a roundhouse palm. His defense (8-11) would be to follow your arm and block with his

Continued on next page

wrist on the inside of your wrist. Your subsequent move (12-15) would be to draw your arm across your body, taking his arm with it, and delivering a chop to his neck. His response is to follow your motion and deflect your wrist to the outside (16) then attempt a back hand counter (17). Perform a small disengagement (18-20) and force his arm down to deliver a strike to his face.

HAND CHANGES

A hand change is accomplished by drawing your free hand up beneath the forearm of your controlling hand and literally wiping your opponent's hand off your first hand without losing contact with him. During the drills with your partner, develop your own footwork by step-

HAND CHANGE

Assume a right stance (1) to your partner's right stance and place the back of your right wrist against the back of his right wrist. Perform a hand change (2-4) and attempt to hit your partner's collarbone with a straight walk smash. He will defend by pushing your hand to his left side. He will then (5-7) attempt to backhand

ping forward or back to complement your hand movement. Practice the hand changes as an addition to your other sticky hand drills. Then mix the drills.

Continued on next page

chop, which you can block with another hand change. Perform a small disengagement (8&9) to get your right hand on the inside of his right wrist and push his wrist to his right to make an opening to his neck. As you attempt a backhand chop (10) he will block with his left wrist. He will then attempt a palm smash to your face. Defend that (11&12) by lifting your right elbow, then perform a hand change.

OPENING MANEUVERS

Opening maneuvers are essentially the same as the two-count drill, but you should remember that an opening can be made at any time by moving your opponent's hand away from the area you plan to strike. The following shows how to make an opening by moving your opponent's hand to either side or by pulling it downward. It should be added that any time you deflect a strike over your head, you have created an opening for a downward smash.

OPENING SIDE TO SIDE

Face your partner's left jab in a right short flat walk stance (1) and deflect his punch to the face (2) to the outside to create an opening. When you attempt a two finger jab to his throat (3) your partner

will defend by maintaining contact with your wrist and pushing your hand across and down. As he attacks (4) with a backfist (5) deflect it with your left wrist.

PULL DOWN

Assume a right stance (1) to your partner's left stance and place the back of your right wrist against the inside of his left wrist. Your partner's objective (2&3) is to pull your hand down and strike to your chin with a palm smash. Instead, when he pulls downward and strikes to your head (4&5), follow his energy with the back of your wrist and direct his hand to your right (6) with a cobra block. Use the opening for a finger strike to the eye (7), which he should block by pushing your hand across his body. He should then attempt (8) a back knuckle strike, which you block by pushing his hand to your right again.

DOUBLE STICKY HANDS PRACTICE

Double sticky hands is the last exercise before going into the trapping hands stage. Since it is a continuous movement, the example that follows is only a hypothetical sequence you may encounter during a double hand practice session.

DOUBLE STICKY HANDS PRACTICE

Begin by facing each other (1), hands at your sides. Bring your hands up so that your left wrists rest on top of each others' right wrist. As your partner attempts a face attack with his left hand, deflect it to the outside (2&3) with your right and hit upward with your left hand. He should deflect your left

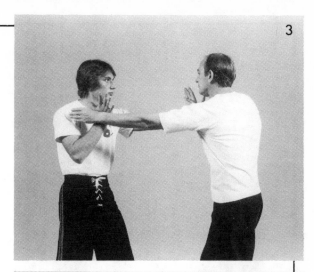

3

hand to the outside with his right. As you counter with a right hand attack to his face (4), he should deflect your hand downward and across his body while attempting an attack to your face with his right hand, which you also deflect downward and to the outside. Continue in this pattern (5) until one of you breaks through the other's defense.

4

5

TRAPPING HANDS

There are two major categories in the trapping hands of Hsing-i: checking traps and opening traps. Checking traps are accomplished with a combination attack or a simultaneous block and counter. In a combination attack, when your first attacking hand is blocked, you use that hand to immobilize your opponent's blocking hand and plant your second strike with

CHECKING TRAP

Assume a right short flat walk stance (1) to your opponent's right stance. Cock your right fist back to your left ear (2) and execute a downward back knuckle strike with your right hand (3) which your opponent blocks above

your free hand in the area he has left open. In the simultaneous block and counter, you immobilize his attacking hand by blocking, and then you strike to the area he has left open at the same time.

An opening trap is accomplished by moving your opponent's attacking or blocking hand and striking to the opening you have created.

his head with his right forearm. Finally (4) while holding your right arm against his blocking arm, step forward with your left foot into an entering tiger stance and strike with a left vertical fist to his midsection beneath his block.

CHECKING TRAP

Assume a right short flat walk stance (1) to your opponent's left stance. As your opponent steps forward to attempt a right punch (2&3) block it upward with your right fore-

arm while stepping forward (4) into an entering tiger stance and striking with a left vertical fist to his midsection beneath his right arm.

OPENING TRAP

Assume a right short flat walk stance (1) to your opponent's right stance. Step into a long flat walk stance (2) with your right foot and execute a downward back knuckle strike with your right hand, which your opponent

blocks in front of his face with his right forearm. Finally (3&4) step forward into a left short flat walk stance while pulling his blocking arm downward and deliver a flat walk smash to his face with your left hand.

OPENING TRAP

Assume a right short flat walk stance (1) to your opponent's right boxing stance. As your opponent attempts a right jab (2) deflect it to your right with the outside of your right wrist. Then (3) step forward into a left short flat walk stance while pulling his punch downward with your right hand and delivering a downward flat walk smash with your left.

DEFENSE AGAINST
TRAP #1

Assume a right short flat walk stance (1) to your opponent's left short flat walk stance. Your opponent (2&3) should step forward with his left foot to trap your right arm down-

3

ward. Perform a large disengagement (4) with your right hand while trapping his hand downward with your left. Finally (5) deliver a right palm strike to the side of his head.

4

5

DEFENSE AGAINST TRAP #2

You and your partner face each other (1) in a right short flat walk stance. Your opponent (2) steps forward with his right foot to trap your right arm downward. Then (3) he slides his left foot forward into an entering tiger stance and raises his left

hand for a downward smash while you bring your left hand to your right shoulder. Perform a hand change (4) and deflect his downward smash to your left. Finally (5&6) follow through with a right palm smash to the side of his head.

DEFENSE AGAINST TRAP #3

(1) Face your partner in a left short flat walk stance. Your opponent steps forward (2) with his left foot and traps your left arm. As he lifts his right fist (3) for an overhand punch and

starts his motion forward, pull your left arm across your body while bringing your right hand, palm up, beneath your left forearm. Finally (4) deliver a willow leaf palm to the face.

DEFENSE AGAINST
TRAP #4

Assume a right short flat walk stance (1) to your opponent's left short flat walk stance. Your opponent steps forward (2&3) with his left foot and traps

your right arm downward. Pull your right arm further downward (4&5) and deliver a vertical fist to his chin with your left hand.

DEFENSE AGAINST
TRAP #5

(1) Assume a left short flat walk stance to your opponent's left short flat walk stance with the outsides of your left wrists touching. Your opponent traps your left hand downward (2) and steps forward with

his right foot while raising his right hand for a downward smash. Lift his left arm with yours (3) while ducking under them and delivering an uppercut to his midsection.

TWO MAN WAVE DRILL

During the two man wave drill, your partner attacks in a continuous wave, moving forward as you retreat. When you reach a designated distance, depending on the area you are practicing in, you move forward as he retreats while blocking your attacks.

Do the drill slowly at first, pausing after each movement and looking or feeling for the opening. When you start picking up speed, feel for the energy in both the attack and the defense.

TWO MAN WAVE DRILL

Begin by facing each other (1) in the left short flat walk stance. As your partner steps forward (2&3) to attempt a downward flat walk smash with his right hand step back and deflect it to your right (4) with a hand change. Your partner uses his right elbow to lower your right hand (5&6) over your left. As he springs upward

When you are attacking, keep the pressure on and don't let your partner get too far away.

At first, use the techniques shown in the pictures. Later, the techniques should vary continuously. After you have mastered the drill walking straight forward and back, the defender should start sidestepping the attack and the attacker should alter the angles of his strikes. The short flat walk stance is used throughout the drill.

2

3

5

6

Continued on next page

with an uppercut (7) you follow his energy with both arms and direct it above your head. Your partner steps forward (8&9) with his left foot while pushing your arms down with his right hand as you retreat. As he attempts a downward flat walk smash with his left hand (10) you use the momentary release to bring your left hand up and deflect his strike (11) to your left. For the sake of this exercise, you have reached your designated distance and it is your turn to attack. Step forward (12&13) with your

Continued on next page

right foot while pushing his left arm down with your left and execute a right uppercut over his arm. When he blocks to his right with his right arm perform a hand change (14) so that your left fist is forward, palm in. (15) He steps back with his left leg and deflects your back knuckle strike across his left. Perform a small disengagement to bring your left hand over his right forearm and push downward (16-18), then step forward with your right foot and deliver a right flat walk smash to his face.

TRAPPING
COMBINATION #1

(1) Assume a right short flat walk stance to your opponent's right stance. Then (2) step forward with your right foot and trap your opponent's right hand. Deliver a willow leaf palm (3) to his face with

your left hand. He may deflect (4) your willow leaf palm upward with his left hand. If he does (5) push it downward over his right arm. Finally (6) deliver a right uppercut while checking his arms with your left hand.

TRAPPING COMBINATION #2

(1) Assume a right short flat walk stance to your opponent's left stance. Attempt a right vertical finger strike (2) to his face and he will block it to the inside with his left hand. Then (3) trap his left hand to the inside with your left and execute a large disengagement with your right. Next (4) execute a downward palm smash with your right and he will try to block (5) with his right forearm. Push his right arm down (6) and across his left arm and deliver an uppercut (7&8) to his chin with your left hand.

TRAPPING COMBINATION #3

(1) Assume a right short flat walk stance to your opponent's right stance. Step to his outside (2) with your right foot while trapping down on his right arm with your right hand. Step toward him with your left foot while raising your

left arm for a downward palm smash. He will be forced (3) to block your smash to his right with his left hand. You may then (4) deliver a right vertical punch to his head while trapping his arms down with your left hand.

TWO PUNCH DEFENSE

(1) Assume a right short flat walk stance to your opponent's left stance. As your opponent steps forward with his left foot and attempts a high left jab, (2&3) execute an outside block with your right

hand. Then (4&5) as he attempts a high right punch, execute an inside block with the same hand. Finally (6) deliver a right backhand chop to his neck.

TWO PUNCH DEFENSE

(1) Assume a right short flat walk stance to your opponent's right stance. As your opponent steps forward with his right foot and attempts a high right jab (2) execute an inside crane

block with your right hand. Then (3&4) as he attempts a low left punch, execute a right elbow block and deliver a right upward finger strike to his neck.

TWO PUNCH DEFENSE

(1) Assume a right short flat walk stance to your opponent's left stance. As your opponent steps forward with his left foot and attempts a low left jab (2&3) execute a right-elbow block. As he at-

tempts a high right punch (4) execute an inside crane block with the same hand. Finally (5) disengage your right hand toward you and deliver a right backhand (6) chop to his ribs.

TWO PUNCH DEFENSE

(1) Assume a right short flat walk stance to your opponent's left stance. As your opponent attempts a low left jab (2) execute a right elbow block. Then

3

(3&4) as he attempts a low right punch execute a right downward palm block and deliver a right back knuckle strike to his head.

4

TWO PUNCH DEFENSE

(1) Assume a right short flat walk stance to your opponent's right stance. As your opponent steps forward with his right foot and attempts a low right jab (2) execute a cupping

3

4

hand and fist absorption with your right fist on top. Then (3&4) as he attempts a high left punch, execute a simultaneous right upward block and left vertical punch.

EXPLOSION

Once you have blocked an attack, explode into your opponent with a series of strikes. This exercise is to emphasize hand changes while maintaining strikes. Begin in a right short flat walk stance (1) to your opponent's left stance. As he attempts a low left jab, execute a downward palm block with your left hand while simultaneously (2) delivering a willow leaf palm to his face. Now hit him with a left uppercut (3)

while trapping his left hand with your right. Circle your right hand out and up and deliver a downward palm smash, trapping his hand (4) again with your left. Next, use a left finger and thumb strike to his eyes (5) and trap his hand with your right. Finally, strike him upward into the nose (6) with a right small tiger's mouth, palm out and thumb tucked in.

SIDESTEPPING

If there is any kind of preference to sidestepping inside or outside your opponent's attack it would probably favor stepping outside to block off your opponent's free hand and foot. Techniques that are difficult to step to the outside of are such things as a hook kick, a long arcing punch or the shorter and faster hook punch. These are best handled from the inside. Then, if you are close enough, throw him off of

1

SIDESTEP KICK

(1) Assume a left short flat walk stance to your opponent's left stance. As your opponent steps forward with his right foot to attempt a right punch (2) step forward at a left 45-degree angle and begin a double circular block (3) with your left hand parrying. Then pivot toward

2

you with a double palm push or kick before he can use his second hand. Again, this is not a rule as there are many places in this book that deal with counterattacks from the inside. It is, however, my own preference.

The sequences that follow show just some of the opportunities open to you by sidestepping to the outside.

your opponent on your left foot while sliding your right foot toward you into a right short flat walk stance and complete your double circular block with a grab on the outside of his arm. Finally (4) deliver a right hook kick to his ribs.

SIDESTEP HAND TECHNIQUE

(1) Assume a left short flat walk stance to your opponent's left stance. As your opponent steps forward with his right foot to attempt a right punch (2) step forward at a left 45-degree angle and begin a double circular block with your left hand parry-

ing. Then (3) pivot toward your opponent on your left foot while sliding your right foot into a right short flat walk stance and complete your double circular block. Finally (4&5) push him into a wall or handy obstruction.

TAKEDOWN #1

Assume a left short flat walk stance (1) to your opponent's left stance. Then (2&3) as your opponent steps forward with his right foot to attempt a right punch, sidestep to the outside while executing a double circular block with an arm grab. Next (4&5) without setting your right foot down, hold on to his arm and collapse his right knee with a right sidekick. Finally (6&7) step up to him and deliver a punch to his spine or kidneys.

TAKEDOWN #2

Assume a left short flat walk stance
(1) to your opponent's right stance.
As your opponent steps forward with
a right punch (2), sidestep to the
outside while executing a left parry
and then (3) deliver a side hammerfist
to his ribs. Pivot on your left leg and
slide your right leg behind and between his legs (4) while circling your
right arm (5) around and over his
punching hand and against his throat.
Use your right arm (6) to throw him
over your right leg to the floor. Stomp
down (7&8) on his head with your right
heel.

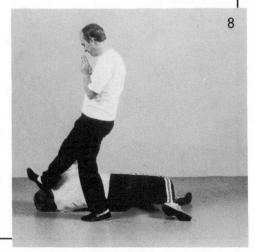

FAKE RETREAT #1

Assume a right short flat walk stance (1) to your opponent's left stance. As your opponent steps forward with his right foot to attempt a right punch (2&3) turn 180 degrees counterclockwise and step away

from him with your right foot. Then (4) circle your left arm back and grab the outside of his right arm. Finally (5) step forward and push down on his arm as you deliver a palm smash to his face.

FAKE RETREAT #2

Assume a right short flat walk stance (1) to your opponent's left stance. As your opponent steps forward with his right foot to attempt a right punch (2&3) turn 180 degrees counterclockwise and

step away from him with your right foot. Then (4) deliver a back kick to his midsection with your left foot. If you have stepped too far away from him, deliver the back kick with your right foot.

CLUB DEFENSE #1

Assume a left short flat walk stance (1) to your opponent's left stance. As your opponent steps forward with his right foot to hit down with the club in his right hand (2) cross your forearms in front of your face and catch his arm between them. Then (3) grab his wrist with your

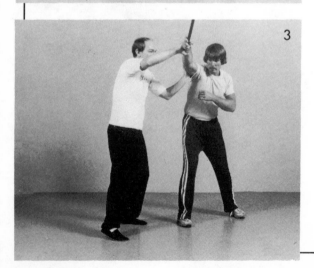

right hand while stepping to the outside of his right foot with your left. Then (4) place your left hand on his arm near the shoulder and use your right hand to twist his wrist so that his elbow turns upward. Finally (5&6) push downward with your left hand.

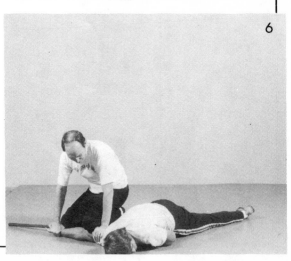

CLUB DEFENSE #2

(1) Assume a right short flat walk stance to your opponent's right stance. (2) As your opponent steps forward with his right foot to hit down with the club in his right hand, block his arm to the outside with

your left forearm. Next (3) hook your right arm at the joint beneath his right elbow. Finally (4-6) bend his elbow with your right arm and push down on his wrist with your left hand to drop him to the ground.

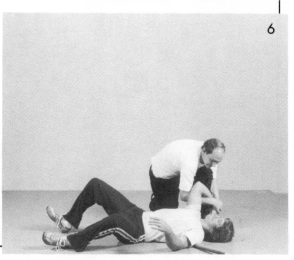

ARM LOCK #1

Assume a right short flat walk stance (1) to your opponent's right stance. As your opponent steps forward with his right foot to attempt a right punch (2) step slightly to your right and chop the inside of his arm at the bicep and forearm with the blades of both hands. Then (3) place your right wrist beneath his elbow and (4&5) slide your right hand toward you to grab the outside of his wrist and place your left hand just above his elbow as you begin to step back with your right foot. Crouch low (6) in a left short flat walk stance as you pull his wrist with your right hand and press downward on the nerve behind his elbow with your left. Finally (7) deliver a right front kick to his solar plexus.

ARM LOCK #2

Assume a right short flat walk stance (1) to your opponent's right stance. As he begins a right backhand chop (2), step forward with your left foot (3) and execute a right outside crane block with a grab while placing your

left hand on his arm near the shoulder. Slide your right hand to his wrist (4), turning his elbow upward and pivoting 90 degrees clockwise. Finally, press down (5&6) with your left hand and pin his arm behind his back while delivering a strike to the back of his head with your right hand.

JAB AND KICK DEFENSE

Assume a right short flat walk stance against your opponent's right stance. As he steps forward with a right punch (2) parry with an outward block with the back of your right wrist.

As your opponent attempts a right side kick (3) execute a downward elbow block with the right arm (4) and counter with a left backhand punch (5) to his face.